WILLIAM STEPHENS

STANDARD FORGINGS
COLLECTED POEMS 1919-1950

Ardis / Ann Arbor

PREFACE

Thirty to forty years ago, during and in the wake of the great Depression, was the heyday of the sociological novel in America. But it was not merely the novel that reflected the economic and political outlook of the time; it was also the heyday of the left-wing and worker-slanted poem. I was then a labor journalist, and I contributed my share of this kind of verse to all the radical magazines and newspapers of the era.

Sometimes, in these periodicals, I would see poetry by one William Stephens. I knew nothing of him (including the fact that the name was a pseudonym), but I liked them. They had an immediacy to the worker's world that many of the genre lacked.

At the same time, or even earlier, I was a frequent contributor to *Poetry*, when Harriet Monroe, its founder, was still its editor (as she was until she died). Here again I found a different kind of poem by the same William Stephens.

I know now that William Stephens was Legare George and I have had an opportunity to read the bulk of the poetry he left behind him, published and unpublished, after his death in 1958. I feel very strongly that it never received the recognition it deserved.

Poetry today has ceased to be communication and is largely solipsist and revelatory only of the poet's own mind and emotions. It has also shed the rhythm which from earliest days was the *sine qua nihil* of poetic expression. Even Walt Whitman had some regard for it. Needless

[5]

to say, along with meter, rhyme has become obsolete.

It may be, therefore, only anachronistic for me to admire the poems of William Stephens, but I don't think so. These poems, collected by his widow, have an exaltation, a heightened feeling, a clarity, directness, and simplicity that put them in the category—if not of great, then certainly of good poetry. They may be echoes of another era, but the lasting and living poetry of the past can have a meaning and a message for the present and future as well.

Miriam Allen deFord

TABLE OF CONTENTS

I. STANDARD FORGINGS

II. SONGS FOR A LOST GIRL

[7]

III. PORTRAIT OF TWO

IV. CLASSIC MYTH

V. SONNETS TO MARGARET

VI. DARK EARTH

I. STANDARD FORGINGS

STANDARD FORGINGS PLANT

All day, all night, we hear, we feel
    the dull, continual thud
of drop-forge hammers pounding steel
to axle-shape and shafted wheel,
    to coupling, tieplate, bolt and stud.

Through long, low blocks of dirty red
    faded by rain and sun
those hammers fall in shed past shed
that, under foot and over head
    move with the plunge of ton on ton.

Their impact rocks the solid ground,
    sand, shale, clay, granite-stone:
in street and house for blocks around
the heavy shock, the hollow sound,
    shake walls, floors, windows, brain and bone.

Common Sense, 1935

FACTORY MODELS

Machines risk change: a clever trick life uses
to put off obsolescence for as long
as time permits flawed bodies not to rust
in scrapheap cemeteries.

Changes are not interchangeable
like factory parts; machines are superseded:
metal goes sooner to the open-hearth
than men go to the grave.

Some men go like scrap, though: standard models
delivered on the same assembly-line
from nursery to board-room, duplicate minds
riveted with the same tools.

Identical in movement, parallel speeds
drive them through office, bank and club until
change, overtaking them, replaces them
as with improved machines.

The Forum, 1936

THE SHIP CANAL

The ship canal unwinds through weedy fields
a long quicksilver newsreel: depth of sky
up which the sun slants westward, sunken clouds
float slowly as white sails in sleep drift by.

No barges ply its course: it ends in mud,
whence maps project an undredged waterway;
but winds have ripped the surface, rain and sleet
wrinkled its film of weather night or day.

In summer, when the sulphur hue near dusk
sinks heat like fever in the flushed canal,
refinery nights leak odors: cracked shale waste
distilled beyond one shore's dissolving wall.

Then as the fields turn eastward, edging dawn,
ammonia pallors rise like mist: the chill
air shivers the cold water; and men find
some corpse, floated beyond the sheetrock mill.

The Forum, 1936

WINTER LANDSCAPE

Late risen, the winter sun glides like a thief
all day behind gray clouds that mask the sky;
wind shakes bare twigs, blows tattered scrap and leaf:
the sun still hides, and never shows its eye.

Its presence in those covering clouds is known
by this rain-colored light in the chill air;
not light, but pallid rumor of a sun
that seems almost as if it were not there.

The day is hardly lighter than the smoke
puffed from those blunt switch-engines in the yards
where cold boys, loading gunnysacks with coke,
run faster than the stumbling railroad guards.

They dodge down alleys, over cracked cement,
hard even to their hurrying urchin feet:
they know that fire is winter's element,
which even in hovel stoves means food and heat.

The New Masses, 1936

MONDAY MORNING

Sunday, accustomed holyday, is over: Christ's
body and blood have been eaten and drunk and,
buried eight hours in the tomb of sleep, are now
remembered, but put aside for practical reasons.
Let no hand dislodge the stone from the sepulchre.

Daily as lysolwater splashed on cement floors
to be spattered around by mops, swept out by brooms,
the sun spills its usual light on weekday streets
inhabited this early only by these equivocal
few men who have just emerged from the town jail.

Monday is better than Sunday: doors are unlocked,
behind which, until customers come, baker and grocer
may be persuaded to give Saturday's stale loaves,
bacon-ends and perhaps a handful of ground coffee.
Another meal, in this man's world, is another meal.

Stirred in tin cans or dented pans under the shadows
in oaktree jungles beside the railroad's right of way,
strong coffee is almost as good as lysol is to wash
the ache from the bones, shivers from the mind that knows
how hard cement floors will be in any man's jail

until hands dislodge the stone from the sepulchre.

The New Masses, 1937

SIMPLE PROGRESSION

I. The Mill

Looking and listening with eye and ear
for birds, alive in woods we've seldom seen;
going with every season of the year,
we have had just that sidewalk glimpse of green
one gets in passing by. Early and late,
in sun or when rain dripped from boughs and eaves,
we've tried to carry through the clockhouse gate
our thoughts of grass, our memories of leaves.

II. The Office

That is our sunset, of which we are justly proud:
a fourcolor film projected on air and cloud,
a continent-length mirage, a barrage of news—
grander, I sometimes think, than a rainbow's hues
that curve to a pot of gold or a Comstock Lode.
Time prints a lithograph now where the rainbow showed:
yellow, red, violet, green, it becomes terrific
before its colors dissolve in the dark Pacific.

Partisan Review, 1936

SNOWFALL BEFORE THEATERS

Walk up one street and down the other
    of this white street where people swarm,
and you will feel lit wings to brother
    the flame you shoulder through the storm.

Not double-arc nor bulbed electric
    nor colored snakelike motions made
in semblance of those epileptic
    gyrations merged in blaze and shade.

Involved in light, that inclination
    from unseen air to streets below
is such as this illumination
    obscurely gathers up as snow.

But who, where flakes of light have hovered,
    goes cognizant of what they seem
shall glimpse the shapes Blake once discovered
    and Jacob laddered to his dream.

Kansas Magazine, 1943

SOUTH CHICAGO, 1937

Here, even in winter, the sun will shine one day
        or another:

Over this packed triangle of city blocks sprawled
        out and warped
southeastward from the university to refinery (from
        the graceful
dominions of knowledge to the barbwired sources
        of ultimate power),
splitting the thin steel shell of cold between us
        and the Florida sky,
the sun will come forth and shine unclouded day.

Unwanted slovenly horde of begging housefronts
        wedged continuously
away from the kept suburban streets of trees and
        hedges,
faded frame buildings cringe eveningward between
        railroads and vacant lots.

Gridiron of warehouse avenues bridged over the
        scum of ship canals
where lakeboats unload coal and iron-ore for the
        southside mills,
are the spouting furnace fires at Republic Steel
        not bright enough for your darkness?
Red neontubes spill fever at midnight around
        beerhalls and the syndicate brothels:
Drink up, boys! forget the starspangled sky and
        the tear-gas bombs bursting in air!

(Here, even in winter, a moon like remembered
        love will shine some night.)

A nightcop's nightstick against a lightpost idly
        brags of the broken heads and the women
        with bloody faces.
A truck's backfiring echoes through the empty
        streets—and suddenly,
fangs unfleshed, the hired animals in uniform
        are upon us,

barking from behind revolver shots in a field
> now
trampled by running men and women who cry out
> and stumble
over slumped bodies covered with white dust and
> red blood
as if by the American flag.

(Here, helmeted in steel, the huntress moon will
> rise one night,
whose bowstring, twanging anger, will drive the
> exact arrows of our laughter
against even the most scornful, the haughtiest
> men.)

Here some day, even in winter, the sun will come
> forth and shine!

The New Republic, 1938

SEWING LOFT

Here, madam, is our summer: heatwave yellow
flooding those dusty windows opened south.
Stale air that traffics alleysmells, pale fellow
of chimney smoke, drifts in to nose and mouth:
on which no man pays taxes. Here are kept
the swollen hours for which our eyes have wept.

And these are the machines at which we serve
apprenticeship to age; these are the chairs
on which our bones absorb the aches that curve
our bodies deathward. Fingers push damp hairs
and watery sweatdrops out of eyes that ache,
pinned to the speed our flickering needles make.

There, madam, on the wall: unlidded eye,
the timeclock stares, computing our spent days;
compounds each hour as it limps goodby,
and points release at six o'clock. Today's
tired eyes look up, hard hands brake wheels down slow:
but piecework cheats the body's cry to go.

The Partisan Review, 1937

SLEEPING BEAUTIES

Enter your houses, draw the blinds
in each room tight around the stale
profusion of your unclothed minds
and your warm bodies, smooth and pale.

The twenty winds of time, outside,
assail, like demons, pane and door:
here let your slumbering wits deride
the changes you have chanced before.

Cold snows that clothed our princesses
in icy garments splashed with mud,
or laid on dark or radiant trees
snowcrowns that now are stained with blood:

Bleak winds that hurried, lad by lad,
our curbstone princes to their doom,
so Jack died of the job he'd had
and Tom choked in a hangman's room:

These ineffectual elements,
Beauties, let clamor at your gates:
custom, that has your heads for tents,
defends its trivial estates.

Let clarion hands peal bell on bell,
charred suns go down, new skies grow deep;
you still in amorous quiet dwell,
who gave your treasures up to sleep.

Common Sense, 1936

NIGHT-CLUB MORNING

What seeing is it, to blink and squint at sunlight
as if the moon made day, as if starshine splashed
with opulence of noon, as sunshowers do,
this blaze of streets and water?

Up! Up! on scaffolds of steel, and see,
unwearied by shining,
the bright exuberant sun, day's luminous phantom,
rise on an intricate city spanning the sky
with swift, immaculate perpendiculars:

The ticking pinnacles of time, their summoning bells,
the clear, aerial trilling of their whistles
drowned in day.

1926

THE EYES HAVE IT

Mister chairman and ladies and gentlemen
and brothers and sisters and fellow citizens:
what is our country now, that we should eye,
and not see red, the fellow in the red necktie,
daughter's dangerous boyfriend at the door,
who talks ignorance about wages and against war
while our true sons boot footballs over goals?

Haven't we cast out ballots at the polls,
sold goods and offices? I put it to you, I
put it to you... The ayes have it: the eyes,
mister chairman, have that intelligent look that comes
at times like this, and not from studying over books,
but from the sound when bugles echo drums,
when dads see red and sons put up their dukes!

(The eyes have a concerted look that sums
up something: not that drunken bum's old pal
the cops dragged up out of the ship canal,
no longer thirsty...nor that tired girl's
who rouged her mouth, who frizzed her hair in curls,
swaying her hips, and hummed, and muttered "Dearie"
for any man to hear who would pay to look.)

The thing demands an answer: Shall our daughters
be friends with agitators, hold their hands
and even cohabit with them. My thought falters!
The idea makes my insides sick and should make yours.
I don't know any more how the home endures
when children mock their folks with smart replies
and wisecracks that a man can't understand!

The ayes have it, mister chairman: the ayes,
the eyes have that determined look that tells
a man's home town is no place for radicals
and college pacifists who disturb the peace.
Haven't we signed this country up on lease,
on business lines? You tell me now: you say
if any eyes see better than ours today!

(The eyes have a deserted look that stares,

not seeing them, at the disused room, the chairs
where daughter placed them, and the unused bed...
What if they should see that seamstress lying dead
on the embalming table, who became weary,
straining to sew shirt-buttons, row on row,
in factories where the eyes see what they know?)

A New Anthology of Modern Poetry, 1936

MEN WITHOUT NAMES

We went to learn who suffered when a chain slipped—
a man not killed: "No, we can't give out names,
against the doctors' orders." Not the doctors—
the industries made that rule: their large givers
started the hospital construction fund,
and certain of their men speak on its board.

We tried the undertaker: "Life and death
may be industrialized, like hours and motions,
but not your ambulance?" Apology
growled in his voice: "They only give us numbers
for injuries—the paycheck number." Well,
we'd get no name for this one at the mill!

"If he was dead, now, maybe—but he isn't,
so I don't have his name." "What do you mean,
if he were dead?" "His name—I'd know it then.
The coroner'd have to have it for his inquest.
I'd have to have it, too. You can't go bury
a man without his name—it isn't legal."

"But if the man were dead, then we'd have learned
his name ourselves. This is a man still living."
We could have given the story up: gone back
and written columns about steel production,
the rising index of employment... No—
we meant to have the name we had gone after.

For men hurt in the industries must die
before reporters get their names. The damage
done to machinery by accidents
is not so great it can't soon be repaired;
what's done to flesh and blood is bad enough—
but damage to the record's serious.

Publicity's the evil. Let reporters
get names and a few facts—the whole affair
is in the papers, spreads by word of mouth
(like rumors that a strip-mill layoff's due)
into the meanest house or bar in town.
Reporters don't get names unless men die.

Ours is a town of workers: usual men,
grimy with steeldust, black from coal and ore;
refinery workers, smelling of the stills;
chemical and cement-mill laborers—men
who earn their lives in two-week periods,
existing on their paychecks, pay to pay.

Men on the average neighborly enough
to be concerned will answer what they know.
Our streets are named for trees (though some are gay
for flowers and some should be named for weeds).
We found our fellow's house on Cedar Street—
and there we found his people and his name.

To us, it seemed appropriate, the street's
being name for the pine's cousin—plain pine boards
were used for coffins before undertakers,
become morticians, used fraternal funds
to bury steel-mill hands in satin linings,
leaving but little for a widow's use.

The man was colder now than the cold steel
he'd handled in the billet-mill that day
before the chain he'd hooked around a billet
to let a craneman hoist it, up aloft,
had snapped and dropped a ton or more of metal
upon his legs and smashed them both off short.

We took his name, with details (wasn't that
what we were there for?) from a slow-tongued son
with hollow eyes, looked at the wordless mother
surrounded by installment furniture,
and two small, foreign-whispering, wide-eyed girls,
forlornly lost—then went away again.

We might as well have given ourselves less trouble
for all we'd gained by running up and down.
If we had known the man was going to die,
we could have saved our legs. When we got back,
the undertaker and the cops had phoned,
and John Zak's name was published on our desks.

Common Sense, 1936

BUSRIDE DOWN MICHIGAN AVENUE

> Found inlings to your bond to
> all that dust.
>
> *Wallace Stevens*

I. Walton Place

It is not cost: opulence reticent
in rose, gold, silver, green of tapestries,
furniture, paintings, Persian rugs, brocades,
prized porcelains of China, ware of Sevres,
plate, jewels, bric-a-brac, objects of art.

Not strict plateglass modistes: Venus in furs,
sheer hosiery limbs in pastel lingerie,
curved breasts of suave flesh bisque, unyielding as
poised facts are priced, under the strapless gowns
and sable evening wraps.

II. Wacker Drive

It is not noon sun
yellowing the buses now that sigh smokeblue
exhaustion at bus stops under these erect towers
that stare the sky out of countenance,
ignoring weather.
Not this autumn wind
rousing inanimate dust and newsprint scraps,
blowing caught skirts of women around
their knees as they lean into it, the lost
dignity of their fooled solicitors
downstreet with bounding merchantile and blown
vicepresidential hats.

III. Randolph Street

It is Lake Michigan's
built-up front footage, paved and overpriced,
bonded and bought.
The cloudcapped towers

(assessed, taxed, mortgaged, sold,
and bought again, and sold,
sandblasted yesterday, floodlighted tonight
under the bluewhite millionpower beacon
swinging its immaterial scimitar
against Infinity in the name of Trade)

bear up the hurried mind with structural ease
from marble foyers sprouting newspapers,
magazines, chewing-gum and chocolate bars,
skyward to tedium:

                    Your timeclock days,
celled behind granite, limestone, tiled facades.

IV. Van Buren Street

Elate, whose wage exalts alternate weeks
with usury of your bondage to the street:

Your unacknowledged link (dread fellowship
and foiled refusal of our common cross)
with every tired mind and muscle
dragged by every aching foot
wearily at the end of every day
homeward from lurching streetcar, swaying El,
bound north or south on Maxwell Street
or west on Lake Street or Division into night.

1944

SOUTH SIDE BEACH, CHICAGO

These days lean backward through slow years: they merge
backward through time with the last time my father
fled to this lakeside and crouched beside these waters.

(Was it only last summer, or the summer
before last summer, or the summer before,
that my grave, careful, pitiful people first,
out of the bleak, immense, paved wilderness of city heat,
block after block behind them, came to this shore
and stood upon this lakeside beside the still waters,
uttering glad cries and laughing with happiness
to rinse the day's heat away in wind and wave
and lave their weariness in lapping water?)

Here, under intolerable sunlight after
the heat of the chase, and so forever escaping
the rioters armed with terror, my father drowned
heartbreak in his black body beneath these waves.

1944

CRY OPEN EYES

Cry "Open!" to the sightless eyes and blind
that look, yet see no wrong. Let misery
beat at the ignorant and protected mind
with fists of gaunt insistence. Let a sea
of tidal anger flood the sun-walled shore
security inhabits unconcerned.
Let tempests of antagonism roar,
that hard soil of freedom lies unturned.

Not against April and its violet:
they still, in this protracted breach in time,
breathe innocence until the heart forgets
man's world in nature's. Rise against the crime
of hunger amidst corn, of hard-wrung pride
made suppliant at this feast of Barmecide.

Common Sense, 1935

A NARROW TREE

What do you fear to see? What is it now
there, at the narrow slant of that bare tree:
the leafless branch that blossomed once, green bough
thick with dark leaves, where fruit hung heavily?
What is it, under that branch, you fear to see?

Is it the shape of death you fear: the shape
of him that was alive, but now is dead?
Is it the taut rope knotted at the nape
where the neck broke? Is it the bent black head:
not host to reason now, since reason fled?

Why do you fear to see, there on that bare
hill, on that cabined hillside, death and death:
dangling in limbs that fought the floorless air;
hunched in that cabin where your mob's one breath
blew out the lamp and fouled the night with death?

Is it the silence in the twilight here
that angers you, until your throat in pain
aches for Gethsemane's tumult? Was it there
magnolias of love without a stain
shed purities that blackened in your brain?

Poetry Chap-Book, 1945

THE OLD MEN

Pay no attention to us—we have used up our day,
departing, we leave you not much that is likely
        to stay:
a burnt-over woodlot, a field of unharvested grain,
this wind-beaten farmhouse, these barns that are
        rotted by rain.
Only the stalks of our love-scented lilacs remain.

We followed our fathers, the plainsmen, the fencers
        of land:
hard slaves of abundance, they left us this desert
        of sand,
these flood-waters drowning your future, these
        desolate scenes.
From acres as dry as the bones a coyote's tooth
        cleans,
we leave you for homestead a shed full of rusted
        machines.

Poetry, 1937

THE WINNING OF THE WEST

I am Joe Grandys: I have gone at night
under the stars until the early light
came faint along the hills; and I have slept
in rock arroyos where the shadows crept
while lizards watched me sleeping in the shade.

Then, when the sun was sinking, I have made
a careful fire beside my saddle pack,
have eaten and put pack and saddle back
on pony and lead-pony, and have gone
across the desert with the setting sun.

Poetry, 1936

or else remote and safe, it seemed, from the
     ingenious explosions, the devastation,
the destructive skills, the technically superior
     defects of civilization,

(how often were children safe, how many by age
     or infirmity were withheld from sudden death?
who went with the wind, riding the tradewinds,
     did they escape the whirlwind's breath?)

we became accustomed to them, got used to know-
     ing that certainly the end of the world would come,
the voices of men be wind in trees, be murmur of
     hurrying brooks, like stones be dumb,

(from cringing to and fro upon Earth and its
     waters, dwelling in depths of despair,
lift up your eyes unto the everlasting hills
     as they vanish in sundered air)

and, dead in the ruined cities, none: not all
     the slain, not those drowned under the sea,
would remember man's infamy.

1944

THE WREATH OF ATOMS

At what proud, trebled cost,
spendthrift of lives at need

(sons lost and daughters lost,
young fathers lost: our seed
spent out like chaff upon
that sevenfold flame before
Evil, its weapons gone
from its own forges, bore
their iron in its own throat)

had we paid out our fee
to watch folly explode
the one peace we could see.

1944

THE SILENT SLAIN

> And each slow dusk a drawing-down
> of blinds.
> > *Wilfred Owen*

And so night came upon them, who had been
like mornings in fair lands.
> > The dusk between
darkness and daylight, when the mind awake
probes its known anguish and the heart's new ache
can be supported: grief is personal.

But guilt infects the membered tribunal
that legislates dissension after death
and gambles with estate: politic breath
defrauding death's elect.
> > The dusk between
daylight and darkness, when the living green
of hill and valley, town and sun-warmed plain
sinks in time's covering night, holds too much pain.

No star for guidance in the cloud-struck sky;
storms threaten, and the weather prophets lie.

1926, Chicago

PORTRAIT OF ONE

I.

In fields of luminous flowers, he had grown
gaunt weeds that showed but ragged blooms to these:
waking the sultry autumn voices of the trees,
came rains that murmured: He is overthrown!
came winds that cried: The day is not his own
to be foregone or sponsored, as he please:
as if the sun, good bringer of release,
had blinded him to seeing where it shone.

For time, exactly competent, assigns
to some this tangled gleaning of their worth;
to others, trellised honors greatly won.
And when the cowards perish, time consigns,
without regret, their sorrow to the earth,
their valor to the setting of the sun.

II.

Disaster's innuendoes weave and weave
intolerable music from despair:
swift as the sunlight shaken from her hair,
cruel as his dark tumults, that retrieve
the fiercely sunken reasons why men grieve
who seize time's fury for a mask to wear
upon the torment of a face laid bare
by words that flay like lashes to deceive.

Under the whirling torture of his heart
no other voice than hers contrives its clear
cold elegies or lifts its hymns to scorn;
no other magics pierce with needled art
the lacerated will that clings to hear
his breath wring courage from a twisted horn.

III.

There was a gradual fire in the west
one evening: he saw it burn and flare

out of the smoke and haze, the truce of air.
The war of sky and chimney sank to rest
and light flowed into color: light caressed
the darkness in his eyes until, aware
of more than flame or bloom of sunset there,
he knew the silent doom his heart possessed.

For now the flood of color ebbed; the light
declined, receding into shadow: soon
came twilight, quiet as the lapse of breath.
And in untender and enormous night
his eyes, uplifted to the lonely moon,
beheld the slender solitude of death.

IV.

And if he glimmer as a ghost, his eyes,
you think, are moonpools luminous with fear's
cold and mercurial radiance; and tears
are phosphorescent on his cheek, replies
emerging to the pallors of surmise,
are dim geometricians of arrears
encompassing a circle, are his years
involved in cycles of an enterprise?

Be not deceived: moon's light is not his own;
no fire is now his own in any sun,
with geometric swiftness to be spun
into expanding mornings. He has known
solar corrosions in a place of stone
and by night's lucid terrors is undone.

Kansas Magazine, 1944
(written, 1926)

JOURNEYING STAR

In Memory of Franklin Delano Roosevelt

Morning its chill and amethyst
reluctance brightens: star and mist
dissolve in deepening waves of amber.
Light pours, unpooled. Mornings remember
bare emblems, images of grief:
cold stalk, wet petal, rime-wet leaf.

Though suns that burnish mists away
obscure Aldebaran's tidal day,
in light that flows like furnaced metal
dew glistens, clear on leaf and petal:
stem, thorn, and blossom, garlanded
above the loved and hated head.

Journeying star! Your zenith gleam
shone over Lexingtons of dream:
splintered shuddering years, and gave us
courage within ourselves to save us!
Shepherd of wrath: our tongued offense,
unstopped, for hurtled innocents!

1945, Winnetka

II. SONGS FOR A LOST GIRL

SONGS FOR A LOST GIRL

I. Bough of Summer

I do not know how far I came
through fields where roses blew to flame,
through leaves the first frost made to burn
from branches where no leaves return.

I dare not guess how far I go
on roads December filled with snow
till starlight made the snow to shine
in barren meadows that were mine.

For snowflakes, falling through the air,
clung white as petals in your hair;
through day and dark I see them cling
like petals blown from boughs of spring.

And all at once your arms are filled
with snowy bloom the wind has spilled
from pear-tree boughs and apple trees
and hawthrown branches white as these.

Beyond your door the sunlight fades
from roads the storm-wind clouds and shades;
but, changeless, you prevail through storms
with boughs of summer in your arms.

II. Autumn Wind

Outside her window the elm tree stands,
tapping the pane till her dream-pale hands
shall take its colors. She understands,
since the wind's been in the tree all day,
changing and blowing its leaves away,
that they must go, but the tree will stay.

Love, should you walk there under the bough
when next the leaves fall as they fall now,
they will go lightly, just touching your brow.

I would have gone so, had I known how.

III. The Golden Elm

When I am borne toward other shores than these
with men who die and leave the hearts they love,
if looking back, I see our golden trees
sway to the blue above:

Not then shall lack of breath compel me there,
or active limbs to cleave the shadowy tide;
but I shall burn my way through the chill air
until I reach your side.

The fatal goddess figured on the prow
will gaze at the dark water and be still,
and all the sad and scornful dead will bow
to love's unaltering will.

Under the golden elm leaves, where they fall,
under the sky no bluer than your eyes,
my self will wander quietly, and call
until your self replies.

You will be reading in a russet book
with sunlit pages and a pictured faun;
a leaf will fall: and, almost, will you look
to see me on the lawn?

Love, will you hear me call, and will you speak
to answer me, because you understand?
Nor think it is the wind upon your cheek,
the breath upon your hand?

But will you come and walk beside me there
among the leaves along the quiet street?
Then all my thoughts, as soundless on the air,
will fall around your feet

till earth and sky and hills, amid the blue
flood of old days up time's remembering shore,
put on lost beauty, and the love we knew
be as it was before.

1928

RAIN WAKES ROSES

It may have been an old poem he read when rain slid down
the dark pane of his window and crept through the still town.

It may have been an old terror his heart felt at the rain,
to know that rain wakes roses and he'd not see them again,

but would gather the cold flowers waves wash on a shore
when his heart, drowned under darkness, couldn't feel any more.

It may have been his fearing that not even cool rain
could wash his heart clean of evil or cleanse it of stain,

and he could not draw the covers and creep into his cold bed
for fear of the night's darkness and dark thoughts in his head.

Else, beyond all of these, it must have been her face
burning through his heart's pain (that fell in that dark place),

and her eyes, swiftly burning through the slow mist of rain,
that made his heart quiet and his mind quiet again,

until he thought: The darkness, and the rain falling all night,
cannot destroy her beauty nor put out of my heart's sight

her heart's utter wisdom and her mind's fire and light.

1927

TO THOSE WHO DREAM

My love is like a gentle wind
that in bleak gardens, winter-thinned,
buried till then in drifted snow,
contrives that summer's roses grow.
A wanderer under leafy trees,
the daisies spring to brush her knees,
sending light showers, where she passes,
of moisture to the shaken grasses.

My love is like a merry song
by happy voices borne along;
her laughter seems the crystal fall
of waters near a garden wall;
like sunlight in the wind, her hair
weaves webs of airy gossamer;
her motion through the meadows seems
perfection only glimpsed in dreams.

My love bestows her glowing eyes
at intervals, in kind surprise;
her touch is like a slender chain
of silver moonlight linked with rain.
Her lips are curious thieves at night,
sly beggars, eager for delight:
but when the morning's rays arise
her lips are still as lids and eyes.

My love—beloved—when she wakes
has eyes as clear as mountain lakes;
under the murmur of her voice
lurk unimaginable joys.
Her breast is gentleness, her mouth
is sweet with odors of the south;
and all around me when she smiles
are portents of the happy isles.

All round me, when she smiles,
are glimpses of the blessed isles.

1927

BALLAD OF A DOOR

The door is locked and bolted,
    the windows closed and barred:
I could break them down again
    if my heart were hard.

"O heart, you are as hard as stone.
    I never knew before
that I could throw you like a rock
    against a bolted door,

could hurl my heart and break a door
    to let the moonlight in;
smash windows open to the night's
    invisible cherubim,

till stars should roof the airy house,
    and in each shadowy room
the moon should weave a silent spell
    as beautiful as doom!"

The door is locked and bolted,
    the windows closed and barred.
But someone speaks within the house,
    who says, "The road is hard."

She says: "The road is very hard,
    but some have gone before
on harder roads than you could go
    beyond a bolted door.

"Some have gone with love and scorn,
    walked with death and birth;
laughed at evil, close at hand,
    and snared a star to earth.

"Eastward is the gleaming moon;
    westward rides the sun:
all the stars will shine again
    when the journey's done."

Beyond the prairies goes the road,
    beyond a western hill
where sunsets burn above the sea
    and starlit nights are still.

1925

TEMPORAL DIALOGUE

If you should ask me a question
    and I should sink in the snow,
there would be only an answer
    that neither of us would know.

The answer sprouts to a question,
    the question grows to a tree
that reaches as high as you are
    from roots no deeper than me.

If you should give me an answer
    and I should step to the sun,
would there be only an ending
    of what was never begun?

The question grows to an answer,
    the answer springs to a tree
whose branches flower in cloud tops,
    whose roots go under the sea.

Poetry, 1940

TOPICAL POEM

We climbed those barren hills by ways
uncovered to the blazing sun;
but when the fire of noon was gone
we looked into the hidden place:

An arid valley, far unrolled,
where silence gathered into sound
to break, upon that stony ground,
its living waters, clear and cold.

Then in the desert birds began
to sing, by that imagined stream,
of conquerors who lived a dream
because they dreamed the death of Man.

Poetry, 1940

HOWEVER DARK THE NIGHT

I.

Being the oracle to whom he'll speak
without response; the silence whence his word
comes back unowned, as if she had not heard
and would not hear again; being this bleak
shape of unutterance whose carven cheek,
poised on the cold, white hand, has not yet stirred
(truth clearly shown, by no resemblance blurred
to what in him confusion leaves to seek):

She is that still immediate grief in stone
whose quietude transcends all speech he'll find
to point the clear, miraculous, glimpsed head:
the loveliness drawn over curven bone
as silently as thought upon the mind
of one amongst the living who was dead.

II.

Should he observe, with eyes aware of time,
December twilights fade across the snow,
he would not turn to watch the bright stars climb
the margin of the night, nor heed the slow
waves washing a dim shore, nor fear the dark
or the gods' angry voices or the doom
of wind and water or that lucid ark
in which the moon's ethereal lillies bloom.

But he would come and look into her eyes
and say: "This troubled heart has loved you more
than its own peace or the uncertain skies
or the last wave that lapses from the shore:
and has but seen, however dark the night,
one star at least still beautiful and bright."

Poetry, 1940

THE DOVES

My love came to me when the windless tide
was ebbing with the twilight to the west,
She said: "Those two gray doves have sought their nest,
that all day long from bough and leaf have cried
and, quiet now, sleep gently side by side,
cradled in silence, with their wings at rest."
She took my heart and pinned it on her breast,
and I sank down and soon thereafter died.

She took my heart and pinned it on her breast:
and I rose up on soundless feet and came
to pour my years like leaves into her hands.
Her breast is sleep and two white doves that rest
with folded wings, and peace that has no name
save on her lips. I wander in dim lands.

Poetry, 1927

PORTRAIT OF SUSANNA

She does not mind so much that sorrow's dark
and shadowy hood should cloak the brow of love,
or hatred's breath blow out the cherished spark,
or death's impartial visage bend above
one's other self, in whom one's self has died,
nor that the thrust of circumstance should part
lover from destined lover and divide
and sever life from life and heart from heart.

She does not mind so much: one could withstand
the pangs of scorn, the loneliness of grief.
She cannot bear that love's accustomed hand
should bear no dream at last, its dulled belief
no longer hear at summer's golden end
pride, singing in the towers of the wind.

Coronet, 1938
(written 1932)

FLAME AND BIRD

There is a flame, there is a bird:
    the fire blows, the singer grieves.
But I believe the sound you heard
    was wind among the troubled leaves:
but I believe the sound you heard
    was wind that stirred the leaves.

If there be pain to make one cry,
    it cannot be for fear of bars.
I think dust blown across the sky
    would be as silent as the stars:
I think dust blown across the sky
    were secret as the stars.

But wind among the leaves must go
    like hands upon a troubled loom,
must find a way from fields of snow
    to fields that would be white with bloom:
must find a way from fields of snow
    to fields of snowy bloom.

Poetry, 1927

PETITE CHANSON DISCRETE POUR CELLES
QUI ONT PLEURES LES MECHANTS GARS

Elise: Mais, au moins, ils ne
dédaignent pas la bouche dont
la salive les a enivres?
Moi: Ils en oublient jusqu'au
goût.
Elise: Eux aussi? J'ai envie de pleurer!
—Remy de Gourmont,
Une Nuit au Luxembourg

Les vierges,
bienveillantes
mais modestes,
embrassent les
gars, pour les
laisser mieux
partir pour
la guerre.

Troubled in March by furious winds that blew
at twilight, blowing a small, scared moon
                  through clouds,
or by midsummer evenings confiding
dew to your hair and coolness to your hands,
they made you meek avowals, whispering
intimations of their disquietude.
They were like tuned instruments
played on by fugitives.

For that war, coming to them, vouchsafed
this curious excellence to novices
for a tenderness, a gift to be conferred
as roses would be pinned by clumsy hands,
therefore, maidens, did you receive them
mysteriously among trees and with kind mouths
discreetly woo their phrases, remembering
others, once loved by other women,
who went away.

Grieving for those, you whispered after these:
"And shall we see them go, see others purge
the wounds like roses burning in their flesh,
who die upon the verge, a day from home,
and never will return?"

Mais les gars,
en suivant les
parfums des
femmes,
oublient la
bienveillance
des vierges.

And they survived your pity, having found
(after days and nights, the mud in camps,
silence intent on earth, sky, men and trenches)
wet evening mingling on the boulevards
laughter and talk, tobacco smoke and scents
of perfumes and cosmetics warm from wraps:
anonymous seductions, casual

and effortless to stroke the anxious pride
stirring boys who shrink or smile,
appraise, deliberate, confirm, amongst the talk
and laughter in cafes.

Et après,
les honteux
parlent tout
bas, comme il
faut aux
pleureuses, et
l'on entend
de petites
complaintes.

From cinemas and porches you return
to reaffirm the gesture of romance,
so much the same to you until your fears,
roused by a mood or quickened by a glance,
appraise, deliberate, confirm, amongst the words
and pauses and replies:

"We gave you...something. You have lost
something!" (A flower dropped from a coat.)
And if they trembled when you cried
against their shoulders, if their eyes
met the disorder of your pride
with some confusion, some surprise,
the taste of such simplicities of grief
upon your lips was mixed upon their kisses
like bitterness in honey. Whence they whimpered:
"We died upon the verge, a day from home,
and were born again; and how shall we forget?"

The Dial, 1919

PORTRAIT OF TWO

THEME FOR A MARRIAGE SERVICE

Could she emerge in blood and bone
    as adequate to need,
she would burn skyward out of stone,
    would flower from a seed.

Could she inhabit nerve and hand
    responsive to her will,
she would assemble sky and land
    as dawn does on a hill.

She would assume contingent day
    and tour illumined night,
a star compounded so of clay
    the flesh breaks into light.

Her voice would be as dews arise,
    her actual hands would trace
their flowerlike wisdom in his eyes
    and heal his stricken face.

And her amended eyes would be
    unanxious of the tide
that bears her body out to sea
    but lets her heart abide.

Poetry, 1927

PORTRAIT OF TWO

Only by certain hours when the moon,
flooding the countryside through leafless trees,
poured down its wintry light upon her face
and wind but gently disarrayed the hair
flung backward from her small, defiant brow—

only by moments when the gradual stars
and she were kindred and her mind became
as cold and as remote from him as stone—

only by these will he remember her
till memory is nothing and his blood,
that once was hers, is dust blown out of time—

his heart being what it was before he knew
the sunburnt desert and the thirst for dew?

Not by these only (for his heart is still
amazed and strangely shaken by her voice,
like syllables of song), nor by the care
that marked the steady justness of her mind.

The traits that so endeared her to him then
are constant and familiar as her name:
the way she crossed a room or closed a door
or, answering, came presently downstairs,
bringing her human gift of loveliness
to him, who waited in the hall below—

Her quiet, sidelong glance, her slender hands
in motion or repose, and her small head
shaped clearly as a faun's head carved from stone—

By these—by certain silences at dawn
and certain hours at sunset under trees
or on a hillside, gazing at the sky
(what did she see that he could never see?)—
by truth like daylight, beauty like the bloom
of bridalwreath and lilac in her room.

But, most, by certain moments when her eyes
were life and death and terror and surmise.

Esquire, 1940 (written 1927)

SUBSTRATUM

Fire masked by falling snow,
love is not enough, I know:
fiercer sources underneath
have that burning core for sheath.

Though the governing heart decree
what the bloodstream's tide shall be,
unaware, our pulses ride
out of ocean's stronger tide.

Not that strength will falter here,
constant in its war with fear,
or your steady household arm
fail beneath time's load of harm.

But the struggles, mine and yours
and the worse our kind endures,
pierce our surest faith to reach
strength not even love can teach.

Passionate, unreconciled,
stitch the garments for our child
with that rhythm ocean gave
life engendered in its wave.

Antedating civil shame,
nurse him at volcanic flame:
rear him at that social hearth
rock-built on the upheaved earth.

1937

PATERNITY

Since you and I do both appear
and go like seasons of the year
that change and are no longer here

but silently as weed and rose
are taken where the year bestows
its burials of silent snows

their shifting circumstance of sun
wind rain bud bloom and seed undone
they come and vanish one by one

then let my body's altered pride
impatient heart ebbed tide by tide
affirm that love the years deride.

Proud body that my love had taken
unfleshed your soul, your eyes had shaken
my soul awake as sleepers waken:

unburdened of worn solitude
flesh singular and spirit nude
ungarmented by you—accrued

new seeds of time in season sped
autumnal to your body's bed
our resurrection of us dead

whereby like flowers from the ground
our buried selves arise unbound
and breathe eternity around.

Poetry, 1937

IN A LOCKET FOR A VERY YOUNG GIRL

To Joanna

Spend not your sighs upon the wind,
let no swift river have your tears,

and be to evil unresigned.
Follow the mood that most endears,

but in no season lag behind,
let night count up on day's arrears.

Oblige your steadfast soul to ply
the colors of the changing sky

to changeless patterns in your mind
and figures never drawn by fears.

Your woven days and nights unwind
in cloths uncut by others' shears:

Enough, that time itself unbind
the knotted thread of all your years.

Coronet, 1938

THREE VIGNETTES

I. No Song

She never wrote a song for him,
    she never tied her heart
with little ribbons made of words
    for him to pull apart.

She closed the windows and the door
    to shut him from the place,
and walked her solitary house
    surrounded by his face.

II. Words in a Tavern

In an oaken vessel pour,
cold and tasteless, pale as lust,
now at last the eseential dust:
take it through the broken door.

Let not every comer think
custom's to be served the first.
This must quench a deeper thirst:
give it to the earth to drink.

III. Casement

We have not caught in any sea
    so huge a whale as Time,
nor salvaged out of sovereignty
    one minnow so sublime.

The world's wide window-ledges front
    on oceans spawning stars,
but Earth affirms the guttural grunt
    of swine at pigsty bars.

Coronet, 1940
(written 1928)

THE FALL OF THE CURTAIN

> In the country of the blind the one-eyed
> man is king.
> *Old Proverb*

Encroaching—warped, invulnerable, aware—
his one sound eye, O nations of the blind:

inherits from thrust heart and ravaged mind
threshold and hands, your voice—entangled air;
assumes, possessive in a borrowed chair,
plate, cup and hearth, dominion sealed unsigned:

spoil of stabbed absence, kingdoms not resigned
to treason, smirking on the ruptured stair.

And they who tolled the summer-throated noon,
and they whom twilight hymned, and they who brought
spring's bloodroot to the winter-guerdoned sky:

triumvirate of childhood faiths and soon
by alien pulse to be coerced, held, caught,
imprisoned in his one glassed lightless eye.

1944

CLASSIC MYTH

CLASSIC MYTH

I. Proem

This wingèd ala-wood I've plumed
with a dark feather mottled white,
plucked from an owl where hawthorn bloomed
in the moon-stilled night.

Black is the shaft and sharp the thorn,
but tipped with silvers of Artemis,
when from the tautened hemp is torn
its quiet kiss.

Into an imaged breast of clay
the drawn bow drives the suppliant's word,
the arrowy phrase that cannot slay
nor be deterred.

II. Odysseus

Ulysses in his cap of clouds
might follow over shattered seas,
with tempests ringing in the shrouds,
past Scylla's rock and Cyclops' knees,
a foam-lit figure born of salt
and phosphor under coral caves,
to bear, beneath that stormy vault,
a brief Olympus from the waves.

Penelope, indeed, might weave
time's colored semblance into song
to clothe the silence at her sleeve,
assuming in her web the thong
and sapling, stiff to foe and friend,
none but a beggar's arm could bend.

III. Artemis

I do not ask, for my release,
Olympic breath to calm the sea,
Odysseus' guile nor Jason's fleece
nor the swift heels of Mercury,
nor, from the blue Hesperides,
the fruitage of a golden tree:

No truth in fables out of Greece
will bear me toward Penelope.

Cold and immune above the wave,
her spearhead tipped with silver fire,
the Huntress follows, queen and slave,
her quarry where the stars expire;
helmet and scabbard, spear and glaive,
ring in a silence like desire:

Remembering the love she gave,
my thoughts are her continual choir.

IV. Theseus

Unwind your thought in thread of gold
and thread of crimson, intertwined:
one end within my hand I hold
and trace your laybrinth of mind.

Through changing corridors your voice
in accents caught from wall to wall
diminishes, while I rejoice
to follow as the accents fall,

down caverns where the timeless day
grows insubstantial and obscure
until, with heart intent to stay,
I come upon you, Minotaur!

V. Postlude

Let the dark heavens have their stars:
    Orion's glittering sword,
Venus' gold face and bloody Mars
    weigh less than that light word
you whispered when the early dawn
came pale as moonlight on the lawn.

Not I shall miss the spectral scope of wan Aldebaran:
I mind not Hesperus, nor hope once more to snare the Swan,
who hear the laughter, shrill and sweet,
of children running down the street.

Poetry, 1935
(written 1928-34)

MEDUSA'S HEAD

Not thus the eyes look down, the eyelids
       close, in sleep or sorrow:
those wan lids droop to shield what no man
       knows; their pale curves borrow,
unshadowed still, the pallor of cold cheeks
       where, coldly curven,
they guard her hidden thought until she speaks
       and Death be proven.

PHOENIX

Earth pauses, hushed,
expectant, at the obscure
sill of light. Time
breathes:
        and now

from cold, white, shining
waves, the clear expanse
of water, suddenly
luminous (lightened from
pressure of winds and
weight of darkness)
springs
        the sun—

a radiant disc, spinning
goldenly across the wide
melodious day;
a flaming wheel
forged in utter darkness
beyond mechanics
and from that black furnace
hurled to burn
along a constant arc,
expanding and contracting
in circles of immediate
light that swiftly spreads
across the blue and white
        choiring
of clouds and sky.

What bird, colored by fire,
by fire fleshed and feathered,
born of the death of flames,
shall spread its luminous wings against that light
and soar in shining spirals,
singing the goldenest song of being
through day's intensest blue
into that fiery round,
that blazing eye?

Kansas Magazine, 1943 (written 1926)

INSCRIPTION FOR AN URN

Invita Minerva

Mistress of quiet music, delicately—
whereto your hearer answers who discerns
in this his true perception of your mind
a multitude of studied instances—
once more your unphrased self communicates
the salt, sharp savor of mortality.

Whence, with immortal emblems armed and free
to reaffirm the dawn, the evening,
midnight and noon, the unpermitted skies,
fulfillment of reality be yours,
and canticles melodious in praise;
let, as from choristors, my lack be psalm.

Whose lost renewal time will not assuage,
let memory commend me to your thoughts
as garlands wither. Ceasing not from song
be nocturne now: your voice had quickened me,
who from the bough where truth essayed to bloom
am spent upon your salutary days.

1926

NOT TO TROY

> There's beggary in the love that can be reckoned.
> *Antony and Cleopatra*

She tells him, and her bright, instructive look
convicts him for the malice on her lips:
"Women dispose their love, whence loss will mock
husbands who falter, loitering at their ships."

He studies her, Orestes in his mind,
stung by those wasps that charm her enmity.
Negation coils. He thinks: "I must prove kind,
for this distortion took its ill from me."

But though he shake his head, his penitence
promoting her to truth, she sees him wrung:
assesses him with grave and curious glance
and fails his honor with a gentling tongue.

Her virtues, coined in scarcer gold than Troy's,
concede no market value to their lives;
what she intends is not what pride destroys:
"Husbands prove able and befriend their wives."

Let sorrow sow him while his speech demurs:
her married graces bloom in his replies.
And while she strokes him with that voice of hers,
hysteria winces, taut behind her eyes.

1944

PLEIADES

Souls from bodies dead
Go up like songs to heaven,
By winter's chilly breathing sped
to the brightest even
of the shining Seven.

Twilight dims the snow
in time's glittering meadows;
frosty whispers blow
shadows over shadows.
Souls arise and go.

From failing bodies flung
how lightly up to heaven:
Like songs by choiring voices sung
to the brightest even
of the shining Seven.

1944

YGGSDRASIL

Earth is a tree, roots thrust
downward into constant darkness
whence the thick, scarred, blackened
trunk arises whole and alive,
completing itself in multiple
divisions of branches, twigs
busied in bright air and prompt
with light, untrivial syllables.

Buds burst, quivering, into these
blue flowers of day, these white
cloud-blossoms floating off
to leave such ripening fruits
as dusk will gather, hanging
now in pure fulfillment
upon the weighted boughs that
droop in the langorous orchard air
of afternoon, lazy and laughing.

Soon the shining seeds will fall
in glittering and distant showers
into darkness, deep soil of stars.

But, Earth, have we not seen
how your frail, topmost branches
soar proudly heavenward, to bear
that one most golden blossom
whose petals are unnumbered?

Around the swift whorl of light
the huge corolla flares, its
petals are unfurled in burning
color above the blue meridian
where floats the immense, clear
flower of shining wonder.

Poetry Chap-Book, 1946
(written 1926)

WIND OF WINTER

Blow your wintry tunes, November, blow
far and clear. Dim crow-shadow
drifts on silent shadow wings
(dimmest image of a bird, the faint
motion of a thought on soundless wings),
skims the twisted fences where
comes now only the cold wind
that blows all day, far and clear,
shrill fifes of winter in the land.

Tired earth, weary earth!
Withered now in field and furrow,
dry leaves rustle, dry stalks lean
where, today, the wind will glean,
where the snow will drift tomorrow.

Bird-shadow, shadow of a wintry thought,
shadow of a soundlessness beyond
the soundlessness of shadows:
crow-shadow, shadow of a withered leaf,
skips, twitches, flutters from the littered edge
of woods where naked trees stand shivering
in the white wind of winter blowing snow.

1927

WILLOW

There is a willow by a river,
of earth and aether sprung, whose green
leaves in the cool air stir and quiver;
for points of sunlight glance between,

dart down and strike against the water
in showering sparkles bright as fire.
The willow like an unearthly daughter
bends over, swaying, without desire,

but cold and sad and full of wonder
to see the furious sunlight fall
upon the water flowing under
her fingers untyrannical.

Poetry Chap-Book, 1946
(written 1926)

THE GOING OF THE MOTHS

All afternoon the moths grow drowsier,
sunning their wings where listless winds delay
their hazards, aimless through the glowing day:
gold motes in sunbeams in the limpid air.

Though clover pasture them like winsom sheep
that browse on languid flowers, one by one
warming their furry bodies in the sun
the weary creatures poise their wings in sleep.

So shall we sleep and, sleeping so, shall dream
all afternoon of poppied harvestings,
dew on our ploughlands, heat intense at noon,
and daylight fading from the tranced, cold stream.
Mothlike at last, we too shall fold our wings
where earth's bruised lands lie barren to the moon.

1945

DAYSPRING

Awake! Awake! Arise!
The golden wheel has spun
from dark to shining skies
the circuit of the sun,
whose constant flame returns
in color from the night,
and now the blue of morning burns,
now the noon is bright.

The shadow of our sphere
is earth's own shadow, cast
above that hemisphere
from which the sun has passed.
From sultry skies to blue
the sun has flashed and gone,
on day's faint borders to renew
the colors of the dawn.

O golden wheel, revolve
on your continual arc
and where you spin dissolve
the cloud, the murk, the dark.
The radiant sun returns
in fire from the night,
and where the blue of morning burns
floods the world with light.

1926

BREAKERS

A white tumult
flashing and tumbling
writhing over black, drenched rocks.

On the beach
they run up to a lapping thinness
quicksilver circling to nothingness
over hard sand.

They slide back
sibilant
bubbled to foam
with a vague sigh
subsiding.

The Dial, 1921

AMERICAN FOLK SONGS

I. Song of the South

We do not dwell in the cold lands:
    under a burning sun
our roses blossom; tall corn stands
    where our blue rivers run.

When winter comes to the cold lands
    our flocks return to the south:
There's many a lamb in the sheep-bands
    whose dam gives milk to its mouth.

Our cattle come from the cold lands:
    we hear their bells from afar.
They graze where a field-tower stands
    under a radial star.

When storms rage over the cold lands
    we are at peace in the south.
Our women give us their white hands:
    we kiss them full on the mouth.

We dwell no more in the cold lands:
    under a burning moon
our cities rise beside white sand
    where waves keep an ancient tune.

Trees stand bare in the cold lands,
    but we have fruits on the tree.
our girls race over the white sands;
    they swim with boys in the sea.

When winter comes to the cold lands
    their cold constellations shine:
we dance to the music of horn-bands,
    we drink of a honied wine.

Our years were hard in the cold lands,
    but life is good in the south:
Women take love in their white hands;
    our babes take milk with the mouth.

II. Song of Communion

Lift up your voices, daughters of the earth:
    bared from the hem of night,
round as the breast you clung to at birth,
    moon releases her light.

Lift up your eyes, you tillers of soil:
    drenched from the wave of dawn,
solvent of sleep, rewarder of toil,
    strides the harvesting sun.

Lift up your voices, daughters of men:
    sing, O seeders of sod:
Loved of the moon that rises again,
    loved of the sun, comes God.

1927

SONNETS TO MARGARET

SONNETS TO MARGARET

> Where the heart lies let the brain
> lie also.
> *Robert to Elizabeth Browning*

I.

They are not here who neighbored me to spend
my unearned days and nights like stole cash,
or slouch to scavenge at an alley's end
for salvage from time's heaped and barreled trash.
Nor am I there who heard them with an ear
indulgent to each fevered circumstance,
met grin with grin and matched them leer for leer,
until the reeling pavements seemed to dance.

Caught in this convalescent solitude,
the cancerous years cut out, foul night, foul day;
nurse to diminished pulse and thinning blood,
and you, once near as health, as far away.
I spell and speel with eyes that brood on flame
the unerased, fierce letters of your name.

II.

See how the summer morning floods the sky
with burning light and slants the streets with fire
that sparkles in each glad pedestrian eye
and glints in gold from towering roof and spire.
See how the trees, their branches lately bare,
have budded forth and roused the parks with green
where leaves and grasses, in the glowing air,
dance with the wind as in some childhood scene.

This life was not accomplished in an hour.
The fathering sun, that nourished root and stem
day after day, spent out its genial power,
and summer wears these garlands at her hem.
So I, all winter bare of flower and fruit,
must also grow and blossom from my root.

[86]

III.

Here in a minute arc of that vast wheel
whose fiery bounds approach infinity
so small as to be scarcely visible,
a pinpoint in that glittering galaxy,
our sun and its revolving planets roll
through space and time unnoticed, without sound;
and yet a part of the stupendous whole:
one flower of light on that eternal ground.

and here, upon this petal of the sun,
this fruitful earth, that bore our human kind,
the miracle of life is not undone:
it blossoms in the miracle of mind.
        And the great stars that pace the unending sky
        are mirrored in the oval of your eye.

IV.

Not in dismay at being old in years,
and with not much ingratitude to time,
I watch a world that slowly disappears:
the slopes of life where I no longer climb.
The shadows of an autumn afternoon
lie all around me, and the twilight waits.
I shall but look my last at stars and moon
before I cross the path and close the gates.

Though it is pleasant to be here and still
remember the long road and how it wound
through field and woodland, over stream and hill,
and toiled up mountains over stony ground,
        yet I am shaken as I stare through time
        and think of the high peaks I did not climb.

1951

TO MARGARET

And all my best is dressing old words new.
W. B. Yeats

You wondered quaintly that I named you friend
(and not beloved?) in my bond of death
against that day when all my days must end
and earth's dear airs no longer feed my breath.
But was there cause to question, be amused,
uncertain, sad, disdainful, or relieved?
Remembering how many have abused
impassioned words, have been by such deceived?

There was a time (as there still is in France)
when friend was but the gentler name for love,
breathing devotion and in hopeless chance
requiring but to serve. This may you prove:
    And like that other tall, proud woman find
    in mutual truth the lover friend—and kind.

1954

IN SHADOW OF SHINING

What is in me dark,
Illumine; what is low, raise and support.
Paradise Lost, Book I

I.

Now that my night has cleared, seeing what day
dawns coldly on this bare and alien life
I here inhabit, I have turned once more
to you, dear love; turned once again to you
who now are not my love, yet whom I hold
possessed within my valuing heart and know
profoundly, as the body knows the soul:
For as great persons in our memory
live on and seem to turn to us and speak
their wisdom to our minds, and to our hearts
their painful courage and their troubled pride,
so you exist in me, in me endure.

And so I turn to you before you go,
divorced forever from my life, which once
you shared, endeavoring to raise and help
from weakness and that shadow in my mind
that led me downward: turn and speak at last
the truth which in my heart is better blood
and flows through my whole being.

II.

Could my mind
have pierced that shadow, as the faintest star
through the dark night will shine, and seen how fear
engenders panic, panic cowardice,
and all urge into evil and unwilled wrong
the heart that harbors them, I might not now,
as now I am, exempted from your years,
be exiled in this peopled solitude.
Nor should I have seen effort, in despite
of an upreaching and acquiring aim,
denied its outcome: like an unsound oak
by lightning struck and from its natural ground

cut down and carried off; or else, among
thick, dwarfish and unequal growth, spared space
for roothold, soil to flourish in if still
such tree can grow.
                           For I might then have stood
once more beside you—not as in those days
made onerous by disproportionate growth
between us and my lesser yield than yours
and sorrier fruitage, but with equal breadth
and stature, grown commensurate with you:
comparable in vigorous fruitfulness
and sheltering leafage, he you knew being gone,
lost on the roads he wandered in the dust
and heat of a dry summer.

III.

                           What is reality?
The sepia print of an old photograph
upon the bureau, where with innocent
and candid eyes untroubled yet by pain
or sorrow or that anguish in the heart
that seems to stop its pulse, your face in youth
just flowering into early womanhood
(calm, gentle, and amused, beneath soft waves
of coppery hair, abundant and that half-
conceals your serious forehead) with a cool,
fresh interest looks out upon a world
dead many years ago?
                           The camera face
framed on the wall: in marriage loved, loved now
in solitude. There, with a larger dower
of goodness, in endurance earned; mature
in knowledge and ability, in strength
of purpose and that more contagious health
that nobler natures own: a generous mind
and gentleness of heart, you seem to move
as if you were alive inside the frame.
And yet you do not move: you cannot speak,
nor hear one spoken word; you do not stir.

Still face, whose actual eyes one day met mine
with a slow, studious look before you turned

away and entered in the stranger's gate
(and by that consequential act disowned
the ineffectual presence of a love
struggling to grow, and on your altering way
went from me like the moon that seeks the west):

These portraits real, and the truth I knew—
that warmth of heart, that breadth of mind in you,
that charm of person: wedded trinity
of dowering virtues twined inside my thoughts
and trellised in my memory, green vine
of knowledge that I shall not have again—
unreal now?

        What is reality
but this: that you are gone beyond recall?
For I have sought you and I have not found
in any place, familiar or strange,
the presence of that being whom I felt
committed to my heart. I only see
from desolate places where together once
we two seemed happy for a little while,
your signature upon that fading day.

        IV.

Not in that shadow, only seen at night
in the night's darkness only, being itself
darker than night: the shadow cast by time:
not in that wind heard only at night, far wind
in the dark night heard blowing time away
(these few torn years) beyond a dying star:
When I am dead, the dust I shall become,
my very dust, in dissolution shed
to mingle with its fathering elements
will know you and still feel your influence.

For even as the constant years have changed
and statured you, deepening in your eyes
their serious aspect aureoled with mirth
and liveliness, and on your brow and cheeks
engraved their several and minute scrolls
of chastening record: harsh or desperate

experience, and toll of loss untold
in any ear save memory's (but there
with difficult exactness learned and stern
discretion known and valued), they have now
encircled with an autumn coronel
of personal grace your laureled head, held high
in every weather: coronal that shines
around you where you go as with a clear
and individual radiance: the bright
unguarded shining of an inward light:

Bright in my life, your clear, continuing light.

1949

HOROSCOPE

Who rest their hopes on hope,
dreaming, will circumscribe their scope:
action will not bear them on
to goals hard won,
or tended harvests ripened by the sun.

Who read in plotted stars
causes of wars,
peace, progress, change: substitute resource
for thought's exacting course
and wield no force.

Fulfillment will not recompense
their somnolence:
although pulse quicken until its rhythm break,
reality not slake
their hearts, who dream awake.

1945, Chicago

SOLE EVENT

Say the thing happened, the event occurred:
say that it was and that because it was,
because it happened at a certain time
and in a certain way, it is important
and is to be remembered, noted down,
continuing into time as time recedes.

Accept it then as fact, immutable,
inevitable, that cannot be undone
nor altered nor diminished nor obscured,
but in the always lengthening sum of things
that have occurred, because it did occur,
has its sole place, existing there in time.

Say not that it was not the thing it was:
the single circumstance, unique event
that it was in itself and that it was
to you to whom it happened, whom it changed
and shaped anew, itself unalterable,
immutable, yourself alone being changed.

No, say that as that one event befell
so it befell: and you, being still yourself,
are yet no longer you. You are yourself
now by the that-much-less, the that-much-more,
it took away from you and added to you:
and you are less, more, other than you were.

1944, Winnetka

EPITHALAMIUM

> I am two fooles, I know,
> For loving, and for saying so
> In whining Poetry.
> *John Donne*

Pity the dead, that lie alone,
divorced, rejected: flesh from bone
dissolved like breath, all breathing done.
Pity the dead that are like stone
but do not pity me.

Pity the stirring child for whom,
still safe, uncancelled in the womb,
this world prepares injurious room.
Pity that hapless child its doom,
but do not pity me.

As the bare oak its fallen leaf,
pity most parents their belief;
pity the grievous man his grief;
pity the drunkard, pity the thief,
but do not pity me.

Pity those old, unfriended men
that house in dark hotels, and when
they sleep, then only live again.
Pity those living dead men, then,
but do not pity me.

Pity the bloodied soldier, slain
to swell a nation's few with gain;
pity the well-whipped boy his pain;
pity all fools that love in vain,
but do not pity me.

I am not dead; and though I live,
I have not whom I may not have:
who shouldered water in a sieve,
pity the grateful love I give,
but do not pity me.

DARK EARTH

DARK EARTH

For Dorothy George Lucas

Sister, the winds turn slowly east and west
over this wide land full of sun and rain:
they wake the sleeping grasses on the plain,
they sway the trees upon that low hill's crest
and even to dust give motion, while you rest
as still as if to be secure from pain
were better than to share and love again
the beauty of this world made manifest
in ways that even sorrow had confessed—
as if life done were nothing to regain
or to be felt as loss and so remain
with weight of this dark earth upon your breast.

Poetry, 1942
(written 1926)

THE STONE

For Dorothy George Lucas

Once before I die
I should like to go
west again where I could feel
how the west winds blow,
see the sun go down,
know the night brings rest
when familiar stars return
to the quiet west.

I should not be long
in the land I love:
I should only stay to see
if a shadow move,
only touch the grass
growing by a stone—
only whisper there, My dear,
you are not alone!

1927, Chicago

THE BOY—THE MAN GROWS OLDER

Why should nature seem to be
less than beautiful to me:
less or more or other than
it was to my vision when
as a boy I thought it all
new and dearly beautiful?

Now there's terror in a rose,
there is strangeness now in those
hidden violets I find
(had I either heart or mind)
growing near the roots of trees
or in shadier crevices.

Now the petaled primrose grieves
if I try to part its leaves;
now the daisies in a field
show the surface of a shield;
and the grassblades of a lawn
are like swords to walk upon.

1945, Chicago

TANGLEWOOD TALE

Look far enough back, you'll see
what both of us may remember:
green tangle of leaf, bush, tree,
root fern in a depth of timber;
red vine-leaves tangled ahead,
thick briars around behind us—
"Brother, we're lost," you said,
"Suppose nobody can find us?"

Two children lost in a wood
and frightened by stormy weather:
nor yet have I understood
how we found our way out together.
You followed me: hand in hand
through barrier bush and briar
we climbed. A road through sand
led home to supper and fire.

Our years have fallen like leaves
that go when the wind is blowing;
and startled, the mind still grieves
dismayed at the sound of their going.
Through tangle of days, months, years,
our voices long lost are calling:
but the forest is deep—none hears—
the darkness of night is falling.

1945, Winnetka

Where dreams Tatyana? Where
smiles Onegin? What cold air
does pale Myshkin wander in,
lost with furious Rogozhin?

Where is Chichikov; and where
sleep Natasha and Pierre?
Is Bazarov, is Rudin
one with dangling Stavrogin?

Where's Akakievich? His ghost
rides with Igor and his host;
Karenina and her dear love
lie with dark Raskolnikov.

Shaken is the heart of man:
Alyosha, Dmitri, proud Ivan,
even Ivan's Inquisitor
beat at Yama's guilty door.

1944, Winnetka

THE UNICORN

In Memory of William Butler Yeats

Stars burn and life's faint fountain flows
upward until the starlight shows
where that white beast of dream had lain,
that by no dream was slain.

What light could pierce those sunken eyes?
At that far fountain's brink he lies
motionless, in the cold starlight,
tonight as yesternight.

And they who plundered one by one
the golden orchards of the sun
stare at the dark and wearily
break twigs from a dead tree.

Poetry Chap-book, 1945
(written 1927)

IN MEMORY OF VACHEL LINDSAY

He who has love and lost his love
    is not to be denied,
though all the birds that wheel above
    sing terror at his side:

He shall go down a trodden road
    that winds the darkest land,
a pack of moonlight for his load
    and dreams in either hand.

For having dwelt so long with death
    he will not be afraid
to feel its cool and quiet breath
    come on him from the shade:

And love will be a word as meet
    as any word could be
to bind the heart and speed the feet
    that take him to the sea.

Poetry, 1931

RHYME AND RHYTHM

Shouting their windy words in time
men pause upon a turn of rhyme
and come in twenty words or less
into a place of windlessness.

Spinning as well their rapid years
they stop upon the brink of tears
and veer within a minute's space
into a poised and quiet place.

1948

OUTWARD BOUND

Now that our sun has fallen
     beyond that seaward strand
where twilight's dim horizon
     still severs sky and land,
quietly out of darkness
     deepening toward the west
sign after sign is given
     as landsmen turn to rest.

Flooding the salt wet beaches
     full runs the tide tonight:
O lone ship straining seaward,
     our slant spars drip with light
above us and around us
     glittering cold and clear
where we set sail together
     with nothing left to fear.

Coronet, 1939
(written 1929)

FALLEN LEAF

A truth I touched but could not sieze:
a leaf came down as light as these
the wind blows out of changing trees.

And it was then as if the skies
caved in like time upon my eyes
and broke my flesh but left me wise.

Like thoughts that fall without a sound
it bore my spirit to the ground
by fear of rooted grasses bound,

and it is now as if the day
bore down upon my helpless clay
till time and terror fall away

like windblown leaves and I but go
through snowy light on leagues of snow
to kneel before the truth I know.

1947

POSTSCRIPT

The taste of death is not the taste
     of loss, like ashes on the tongue;
nor waste of breath in words, nor waste
     of tears from eye and eyelid sprung:
it is to sit, and look, and look,
seeing neither lamp nor book.

1950, Chicago

BIOGRAPHICAL NOTE

WILLIAM STEPHENS, 1895-1958

William Stephens was the pen-name of Frank Legare George, born in Salt Lake City, Utah, in 1895, but shortly thereafter going with his family to San Francisco. There he attended elementary school, but left high school after three months. He and his family lived through the earthquake of 1906, and at that time moved to southern California because of the destruction of his father's business. The elder Frank George not only sold pianos but was also the inventor of a patented piano action and actually built two grand pianos with his own action in them.

In Legare's fifteenth year—he was always called that to distinguish him from his father—he ran away from home and lived for about fifteen months in Ontario, California, where he became apprenticed to a printer and learned not only to set type, run a press, but became an expert proofreader and editor. On his return home, his family placed him in the George Junior Republic, an institution for "wayward youth." There the wife of the director became personally interested in his talents, got a job for him in the school library, and urged him to send his poetry to such men as Randolph Bourne and Edwin Arlington Robinson, who in turn encouraged him to continue writing poetry.

Many of the young literary set in San Francisco of 1917 felt much the same about the First World War as did the youth of recent years during Viet Nam, and so when Legare George was drafted, he appealed for alternate service as a conscientious objector, offering one of his earlier poems as proof of his beliefs. He was assigned to the branch of the Medical Corps stationed in Lyons, France, only a few weeks before the Armistice. There he was put in charge of thirty-two beds in the Army hospital during the flu epidemic. Evenings he spent in a bookstore in the town center, and the bookstore proprietor offered to teach him correct, Parisian French. Legare learned to speak a fluent French, and when the United States government—unable to provide transportation for all the returning soldiers—offered six weeks in Paris or four months in a French university, Legare chose to go to Grenoble, where he exchanged English lessons with Russian and French students.

On his return to the States, he was for a time in New York, then in Chicago, where he held various jobs as reporter and began writing and publishing distinguished verse. His first poem, the "Petit Chanson Discrete," to be published appeared in 1919 in

The Dial, edited by Marianne Moore, and many of his poems appeared in the 1920s in Poetry, when it was edited by Harriet Monroe. The latter arranged poetry readings for him in the Chicago area.

In the 1930s during the Great Depression, he wandered jobless for a while through the Midwest, learning the ways of hobo jungles and town jails, as celebrated in his remarkable poem, "Monday Morning." In the late 1930s he was also an editor of one of the CIO's organizing newspapers, *The People's Press,* in Indiana Harbor, and became labor correspondent for Gary, East Chicago, and other steel towns for *The Chicago Daily News.* Much of his best poetry is written out of this experience. He continued, however, all his life to write poetry, not only on socially-conscious subjects, but on lyrical themes.

His last years were spent editing a dictionary of French scientific terms and their English equivalents with his sister, Dr. Gladys George, at the University of California, Berkeley.

He died in Chicago, in February of 1958, at the age of 63.